Wet Wags

by William Overturf
illustrated by Jamie Smith

Practice Decodable 39

McGraw Hill Education

Bothell, WA • Chicago, IL • Columbus, OH • New York, NY

MHEonline.com

Send all inquiries to:
McGraw-Hill Education
8787 Orion Place
Columbus, OH 43240

ISBN: 978-0-02-133167-3
MHID: 0-02-133167-7

Printed in China.

8 9 10 11 12 DSS 27 26 25 24 23

The kids and Wags ran.

"I win!" said Wes.

Wet drops fell.
Wes and Jan went in.

"I wish I ran fast," said Jan.
"I am glad I did not get wet!"

"I left Wags!" said Jan.
"I will get him."

Wags was back.

"I got wet," said Jan.

Wags jumped on Wes.
"And I got wet," grinned Wes.